The Marriage Mystery

AN ANALOGY OF CHRIST AND THE CHURCH TO A MAN AND HIS BRIDE

BY LOUVENIA DUNCAN

Palmetto Publishing Group
Charleston, SC

The Marriage Mystery
Copyright © 2020 by Louvenia Duncan
All rights reserved

No portion of this book may be reproduced, stored in a retrieval system, or transmitted in any form by any means–electronic, mechanical, photocopy, recording, or other except for brief quotations in printed reviews, without prior permission of the author.

First Edition

Printed in the United States

ISBN-13: 978-1-64990-311-2
ISBN-10: 1-64990-311-1

Dedicated to Mother, Hattie Mae Duncan, December 18, 1929- October 9, 2018.

Ephesians 5:29-32 [1]

"29 For no man ever yet hated his own flesh; but nourisheth and cherisheth it, even as the Lord the church: 30 For we are members of his body, of his flesh, and of his bones. 31 For this cause shall a man leave his father and mother, and shall be joined unto his wife, and they two shall be one flesh. 32 This is a great mystery: but I speak concerning Christ and the church." [2]

---

1 The Holy Bible, King James Version
2 Ibid

Introduction

Through the eyes of the Holy Spirit, the Lord revealed to me the similarities between the customary steps to marriage in most societies, and the spiritual steps to marriage between Christ and His Bride. I am endeavoring to express it in this brief analysis.

Selected - Chosen

In many customs, the husband selects his wife out of many, as the one he desired. Jesus choses his bride from the foundation of the world as the apple of his eyes. The church is the Bride of Christ.

John 15:16 [3]

> *"Ye have not chosen me, but I have chosen you, and ordained you, that ye should go and bring forth fruit, and that your fruit should remain: that whatsoever ye shall ask of the Father in my name, he may give it you."* [4]

---

3 Ibid
4 Ibid

The Courting - The Drawing

The husband then courts the wife and wins her heart. He charms her.

Jesus draws His bride to him with loving kindness. He attracts her with an everlasting love. He draws each individual to him with blessings, revelations, love, compassion, intimacy and the works of the Holy Spirit.

John 6:44

> ***"No man can come to me, except the Father which hath sent me draw him: and I will raise him up at the last day."*** [5]

---

[5] Ibid

The Proposal – The Invitation

The husband proposes to his love and asks her to marry him. He wants to be with her until death. Jesus invites us to come to him. He wants us to commit our hearts to him. This bond will last through eternity!

St. Matthew 11:28-30

> *"Come to me, all you who are weary and burdened, and I will give you rest. 29 take my yoke upon you and learn from me, for I am gentle and humble in heart, and you will find rest for your souls. 30 for my yoke is easy and my burden is light."*[6]

---

[6] Ibid

The Acceptance of the Proposal - Repentance

The bride says, "Yes, I will marry you." In essence she is saying, "I will change my life to be with you." "I will give up being single to become married." "I pledge my love to you until death."

Christ's Bride says to Him, "Yes, I repent of my sins." "I will change my ways." "I will submit my life to you and live with you throughout eternity." Repentance means to change your mind. Merriam-Webster defines it as, "1. to turn from sin and dedicate oneself to the amendment of one's life. 2. to feel regret or contrition."[7]

Acts 2:38

> ***"Then Peter said unto them, Repent, and be baptized every one of you in the name of Jesus Christ for the remission of sins, and ye shall receive the gift of the Holy Ghost."***[8]

Even this depicts the "Yes answer – repent," "the wedding ceremony – baptism," and the consummation – "Be filled with the Holy Spirit."

---

[7] Merriam-Webster.com, 2019. https://www.merriam-webster.com/dictionary/repent
[8] Ibid

The Wedding Ceremony – The Baptism

Baptism is a public declaration of your change and commitment to Christ.

The wedding ceremony is a public declaration of your decision to marry and commit to your spouse. Christianity.com explains, "If the meaning of baptism could be boiled down to one word, that word would be identification. Baptism speaks primarily of a personal, public identification with Jesus Christ."[9]

We are baptized in the name Lord Jesus Christ (Acts 2:38), because HE IS THE GROOM TO THE CHURCH. This is uncomfortable for some men because the Church is a feminine gender. However, it is spiritual. Mystically we are all placed in the Church, the Bride of Christ. Whether male or female we are a part of the Church. Collectively, it is the feminine companion of Christ. This is spiritual. At the wedding ceremony, the bride walks down the aisle to meet her husband at the altar. Have you ever noticed an official baptism where the Believer walks down into the pool to be joined to Christ? It is a beautiful illustration of marriage.

---

[9] Christianity.com, "What *is Baptism? It's Meaning & Importance in Christianity.*" *Christianity.com 2019.* https://www.christianity.com/jesus/following-jesus/baptism/what-does-baptism-mean.html (Retrieved on August 24, 2019).

The Vows - The Covenant

The bride and the groom say their "I do's," at the altar. We say, "I Do," at baptism when we are asked if we believe in the death, burial and resurrection of our Lord and Savior Jesus Christ. Both are verbal commitments to covenants.

The Consummation – Receiving the Holy Spirit

Often after the ceremony, the married couple goes on a honeymoon to consummate their union. They come together as one. The two become one flesh. The union is sealed. The Believer is united with Christ through the infilling of the Holy Spirit. The two become one,

1 Cor. 6:17
> *"But he that is joined unto the Lord is one spirit."* [10]

Ephesians 1:13
> *"In Christ ye also trusted after ye heard the word of truth, the Gospel of your salvation, in Whom also after ye believed, ye were sealed with that holy Spirit of promise."* [11]

---

10 Ibid
11 Ibid

Conception – Bearing Fruit

The bride and groom continue in intimacy and the bride receives his seed and bears children. Through the Holy Spirit, we conceive the fruit of the Spirit and we bear fruit for the Kingdom of God.

Galatians 5:22

But the fruit of the Spirit is love, joy, peace, forbearance, kindness, goodness, faithfulness, 23 gentleness and self-control. Against such things there is no law.[12]

---

12 Ibid

The Family – The Church

The bride and her husband build a family together on earth. The Believer and Christ build a spiritual family – the church.

Ephesians 5:30

> *"For we are members of his body, of his flesh, and of his bones."[13]*

Traditionally, through marriage, the wife has a right to her husband's inheritance on earth. She has taken on his NAME. That NAME gives her rights to many things.

Through salvation in the name of JESUS, we now have a right to the inheritance of Christ. God has always dealt with people and their names. Now, we must take on the name of Jesus Christ. This gives us the right to enter heaven, his home. God is looking for the name. It gives us the legal right to all that salvation offers.

Galatians 3:29

> *"And if ye be Christ's, then are ye Abraham's seed and heirs according to the promise."[14]*

---

13 Ibid
14 Ibid

Notes of Interest

A. John the Baptist was the best man that ushered Christ to the altar to meet his bride. He stood with him until his time was up and his mission was complete.

St. John 3:29
> ***"The bride belongs to the bridegroom. The friend who attends the bridegroom waits and listens for him, and is full of joy when he hears the bridegroom's voice. That joy is mine, and it is now complete."***[15]

B. Just as helpers assist the bride with getting dressed for her wedding. Believers customarily assist the baptism candidate with getting dressed for baptism.
C. Through Christ we have a legal right to the Kingdom of God and Heaven. What we lost in Adam, we recovered in Christ.

---

15 Ibid

Conclusion

There are many mysteries in the Word of God. We should aspire to learn them, asking the Holy Spirit to reveal them to us as we walk in wisdom and the leading of God.

Bibliography

Christianity.com

Merriam-Webster.com, 2019.

https://www.me rriam-webster.com/dictionary/repent

The Holy Bible, King James Version

www.ingramcontent.com/pod-product-compliance
Lightning Source LLC
LaVergne TN
LVHW020006080526
838200LV00081B/4473